ASTERIX AND THE GOTHS

TEXT BY GOSCINNY

DRAWINGS BY UDERZO

TRANSLATED BY ANTHEA BELL AND DEREK HOCKRIDGE

HODDER DARGAUD
LONDON SYDNEY AUCKLAND

ASTERIX IN OTHER COUNTRIES

Australia	Hodder Dargaud, 2 Apollo Place, Lane Cove, New South Wales 2066, Australia
Austria	Delta Verlag, Postfach 1215, 7 Stuttgart 1, West Germany
Belgium	Dargaud Bénélux, 3 rue Kindermans, 1050 Brussels, Belgium
Brazil	Record Distribuidora, Rua Argentina 171, 20921 Rio de Janeiro, Brazil
Canada	Dargaud Canada, 307 Benjamin Hudon, St Laurent, Montreal H4N 1J1, Canada
Denmark	Serieforlaget A/S (Gutenberghus Group), Vognmagergade 11, 1148 Copenhagen K, Denmark
Esperanto	Delta Verlag, Postfach 1215, 7 Stuttgart 1, West Germany
Finland	Sanoma Corporation, P.O. Box 107, 00381 Helsinki 38, Finland
France	Dargaud Editeur, 12 Rue Blaise Pascal, 92201 Neuilly sur Seine, France
	(titles up to and including Asterix in Belgium)
	Les Editions Albert René, 81 Avenue Marceau, 75116 Paris, France
	(Asterix and the Great Divide, Asterix and the Black Gold, Asterix and Son)
Germany, West	Delta Verlag, Postfach 1215, 7 Stuttgart 1, West Germany
Holland	Dargaud Bénélux, 3 rue Kindermans, 1050 Brussels, Belgium
	(Distribution) Van Ditmar b.v., Oostelijke Handelskade 11, 1019 BL, Amsterdam, Holland
Hong Kong	Hodder Dargaud, c/o United Publishers Book Services, Stanhope House, 13th Floor, 734 King's Road, Hong Kong
Hungary	Nip Forum, Vojvode Misica 1-3, 2100 Novi Sad, Yugoslavia
India	*(Hindi)* Gowarsons Publishers Private Ltd, Gulab House, Mayapuri, New Delhi 110 064, India
Indonesia	Penerbit Sinar Harapan, J1. Dewi Sartika 136D, Jakarta Cawang, Indonesia
Israel	Dahlia Pelled Publishers, 5 Hamekoubalim St, Herzeliah 46447, Israel
Italy	Dargaud Italia, Via M. Buonarroti 38, 20145 Milan, Italy
Latin America	Grijalbo-Dargaud S.A., Deu y Mata 98-102, Barcelona 29, Spain
New Zealand	Hodder Dargaud, P.O. Box 3858, Auckland 1, New Zealand
Norway	A/S Hjemmet (Gutenburghus Group), Kristian den 4des gt 13, Oslo 1, Norway
Portugal	Meriberica, Avenida Alvares Cabral 84-1° Dto, 1296 Lisbon, Portugal
Roman Empire	*(Latin)* Delta Verlag, Postfach 1215, 7 Stuttgart 1, West Germany
Southern Africa	Hodder Dargaud, P.O. Box 548, Bergvlei, Sandton 2012, South Africa
Spain	Grijalbo-Dargaud S.A., Deu y Mata 98-102, Barcelona 29, Spain
Sweden	Hemmets Journal Forlag (Gutenberghus Group), Fack, 200 22 Malmö, Sweden
Switzerland	Interpress Dargaud S.A., En Budron B, 1052 Le Mont/Lausanne, Switzerland
Turkey	Kervan Kitabcilik, Basin Sanayii ve Ticaret AS, Tercuman Tesisleri, Topkapi-Istanbul, Turkey
USA	Dargaud Publishing International Ltd, 2 Lafayette Court, Greenwich, Conn. 06830, USA
Wales	*(Welsh)* Gwasg Y Dref Wen, 28 Church Road, Whitchurch, Cardiff, Wales
Yugoslavia	Nip Forum, Vojvode Misica 1-3, 2100 Novi Sad, Yugoslavia

Asterix and the Goths

ISBN 0 340 18491 4 (cased)
ISBN 0 340 20295 5 (paperbound)

First published in Great Britain 1974 (cased)
Tenth impression 1985

First published in Great Britain 1976 (paperbound)
Twelfth impression 1986

Published by Hodder Dargaud Ltd,
Mill Road, Dunton Green, Sevenoaks, Kent TN13 2YJ

Printed in Belgium by Henri Proost et Cie, Turnhout

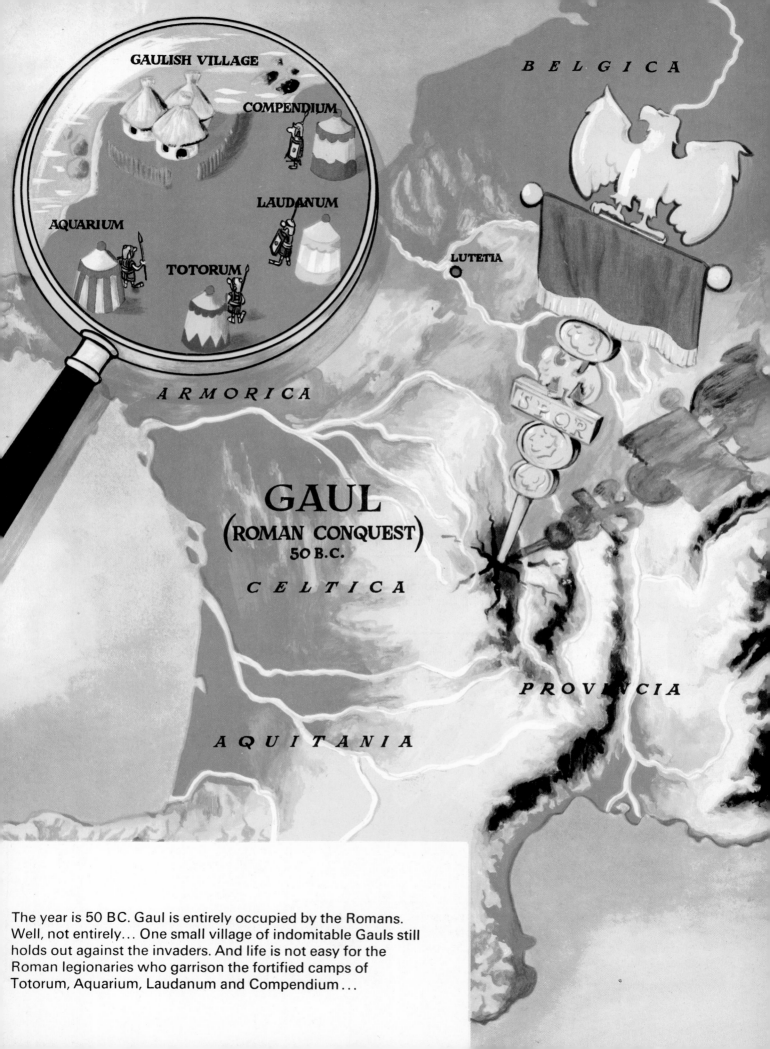

GAULISH VILLAGE

COMPENDIUM

LAUDANUM

AQUARIUM

TOTORUM

ARMORICA

BELGICA

LUTETIA

SPQR

GAUL
(ROMAN CONQUEST)
50 B.C.

CELTICA

PROVINCIA

AQUITANIA

The year is 50 BC. Gaul is entirely occupied by the Romans. Well, not entirely… One small village of indomitable Gauls still holds out against the invaders. And life is not easy for the Roman legionaries who garrison the fortified camps of Totorum, Aquarium, Laudanum and Compendium…

a few of the Gauls

Asterix, the hero of these adventures. A shrewd, cunning little warrior; all perilous missions are immediately entrusted to him. Asterix gets his superhuman strength from the magic potion brewed by the druid Getafix...

Obelix, Asterix's inseparable friend. A menhir delivery-man by trade; addicted to wild boar. Obelix is always ready to drop everything and go off on a new adventure with Asterix — so long as there's wild boar to eat, and plenty of fighting.

Getafix, the venerable village druid. Gathers mistletoe and brews magic potions. His speciality is the potion which gives the drinker superhuman strength. But Getafix also has other recipes up his sleeve...

Cacofonix, the bard. Opinion is divided as to his musical gifts. Cacofonix thinks he's a genius. Everyone else thinks he's un-speakable. But so long as he doesn't speak, let alone sing, everybody likes him...

Finally, Vitalstatistix, the chief of the tribe. Majestic, brave and hot-tempered, the old warrior is respected by his men and feared by his enemies. Vitalstatistix himself has only one fear; he is afraid the sky may fall on his head tomorrow. But as he always says, 'Tomorrow never comes.'

IN THE GAULISH VILLAGE WHERE OUR HEROES LIVE, GETAFIX THE DRUID IS BUSY PREPARING FOR HIS VISIT TO THE FOREST OF THE CARNUTES, WHERE THE DRUIDS HOLD THEIR ANNUAL CONFERENCE TO COMPARE NOTES, MEET OLD FRIENDS, AND HOLD A CONTEST TO ELECT THE DRUID OF THE YEAR...

TRALALA ♪♪♪ TRALALA!

I'M WORRIED, GETAFIX. IT'S A LONG AND DANGEROUS ROAD TO THE FOREST OF THE CARNUTES...

NONSENSE!

LET ME ESCORT YOU GETAFIX!

ASTERIX, YOU KNOW QUITE WELL THAT NON-DRUIDS AREN'T ALLOWED AT THE CONFERENCE!

I'LL GO TO THE EDGE OF THE FOREST WITH YOU AND WAIT FOR YOU THERE...

OH, VERY WELL, IF YOU INSIST

CAN I COME TOO? MENHIRS ARE OUT OF SEASON AT THE MOMENT.

I WILL NOW SING A SONG OF FAREWELL!

OH NO, YOU WON'T! OH NO, YOU WON'T! OH NO, YOU WON'T!

POF! POF! POF!

6

WHILE THESE SERIOUS FRONTIER INCIDENTS ARE TAKING PLACE, OUR FRIENDS ARE ON THEIR WAY TO THE FOREST OF THE CARNUTES...

WE'LL SOON BE THERE. YOU SEE, IT WAS QUITE AN UNEVENTFUL JOURNEY!

BETTER SAFE THAN SORRY...

I'M A BIT PECKISH...

OH! WHAT A PLEASANT SURPRISE!

A WILD BOAR?!

FRIENDS, LET ME INTRODUCE YOU TO MY OLD FRIEND AND COLLEAGUE, THE BRITISH DRUID VALUADDETAX!

OH, I SAY! DELIGHTED, I'M SURE!

COME ALONG, VALUADDETAX! I'M GOING TO AMAZE YOU WITH MY DRUIDICAL PROWESS!

WAIT TILL YOU SEE MINE, OLD BOY!

HALT! WHO GOES THERE?

A ROMAN PATROL!

SHALL WE GET THEM?

NO, NO, OBELIX. WHILE THE CONFERENCE IS ON THERE'S A TRUCE WITH THE ROMANS.

LET US PASS, DECURION. WE ARE DRUIDS GOING TO THE FOREST OF THE CARNUTES.

THAT'S YOUR STORY. JUST PROVE IT!

PROVE THAT WE'RE REAL DRUIDS? NOTHING SIMPLER! WE'LL SHOW YOU OUR MAGIC POWERS...

LET ME, GETAFIX! BE A SPORT!

OH, VERY WELL...

I NEED A VOLUNTEER.

LEGIONARY CADAVERUS! YOU'RE VOLUNTEERING!

?

WOULD YOU EAT THESE HERBS, PLEASE?

SCRUNCH! SCRUNCH!

WELL, WHERE'S THIS 'ERE MAGIC, THEN?

JUST ASK YOUR LEGIONARY TO SAY SOMETHING...

SAY SOMETHING!

HEE-HAW!

HA! HA! HE CAN'T SPEAK ANY MORE, HE CAN ONLY BRAY HO! HO! HO!

IT HASN'T MADE THAT MUCH DIFFERENCE!

?

HA! HA! HI! HI! HI! HO! HO!

ALL RIGHT, YOU CAN PASS. YOU'RE REAL DRUIDS. WE'RE CHECKING UP BECAUSE A HORDE OF GOTHS HAS CROSSED THE FRONTIER. THEY'VE BEEN SEEN IN THIS AREA.

HEE-HAW!

SILENCE IN THE RANKS! FORWARD MARCH!

9

THE FOREST OF THE CARNUTES IS SWARMING WITH DRUIDS IN MERRY MOOD, ALL DELIGHTED TO SEE EACH OTHER AGAIN...

EVERY OAK TREE IS FULL OF DRUIDS HARD AT WORK CUTTING MISTLETOE WITH THEIR SICKLES...

SNIP! SNIP! SNIP!

OOOOUCH! THAT'S MY FINGER!

SWISH!

THEY TALK SHOP, THEY DISCUSS SPELLS...

YES, MY DEAR FELLOW, I PICKED UP THIS SICKLE IN A LITTLE SHOP IN DARIORIGUM! LOOK, IT'S GOT A SAFETY-CATCH.

SO THEN, OLD MAN, HEY PRESTO! I TURNED HIM INTO A MENHIR!

CLACLACLAC

THEY EVEN INDULGE IN JOKES AND PUNS... IN SHORT, THEY ARE HAVING A GOOD TIME.

THIS FOOD'S A BIT SICKLE-Y!

PASS ME THE CELT!

IT MUST BE HIS GAUL BLADDER!

MENHIR A TRUE WORD IS SPOKEN IN JEST!

THEN, AFTER THE GREAT BANQUET...

SILENCE, BROTHERS, SILENCE!

CLANG! CLANG!

CLANG!

BROTHER DRUIDS, THE TIME HAS COME FOR US TO BEGIN OUR GREAT CONTEST TO EVALUATE NEW METHODS AND ELECT THE DRUID OF THE YEAR...

AND WHILE THE DRUIDS PREPARE THEIR MAGIC POTIONS...

...GREEDY EYES ARE WATCHING THEM...

Now comes the interesting part!

THINGS ARE GETTING COMPLICATED. NOT ONLY HAVE WE LOST TIME, BUT THE ROMANS WILL BE AFTER US NOW!

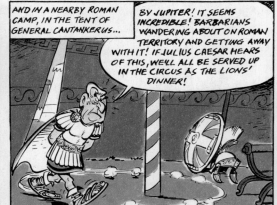

AND IN A NEARBY ROMAN CAMP, IN THE TENT OF GENERAL CANTANKERUS...

BY JUPITER! IT SEEMS INCREDIBLE! BARBARIANS WANDERING ABOUT ON ROMAN TERRITORY AND GETTING AWAY WITH IT! IF JULIUS CAESAR HEARS OF THIS, WE'LL ALL BE SERVED UP IN THE CIRCUS AS THE LIONS' DINNER!

AYE, GENERAL! THE PATROL IS BACK!

SEND THE LEADER IN!

AYE, GENERAL! WE FOUND THE HORDE OF BARBARIANS, BUT WE WERE DEFEATED.

TELL ME WHAT THIS HORDE WAS LIKE.

THERE WAS A FAT ONE AND A LITTLE ONE!

I'LL DRAW YOU A PICTURE...

GET COPIES OF THIS PICTURE MADE AND HAVE THEM SENT TO EVERY CAMP IN THE AREA!

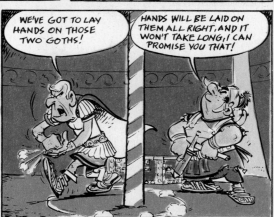

WE'VE GOT TO LAY HANDS ON THOSE TWO GOTHS!

HANDS WILL BE LAID ON THEM ALL RIGHT, AND IT WON'T TAKE LONG, I CAN PROMISE YOU THAT!

RUNNERS SET OFF IN ALL DIRECTIONS...

...AND SOON AFTERWARDS.

SOMEONE'S COMING!

LET'S CLIMB THIS TREE!

16

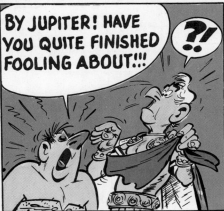

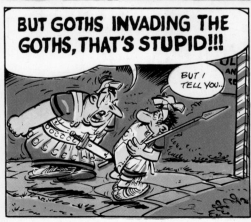

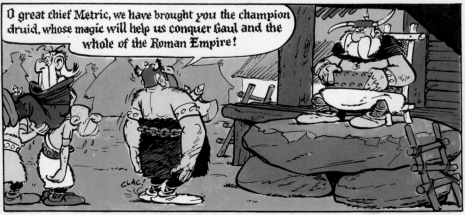

In there!

I'VE HAD JUST ABOUT ENOUGH OF THIS! COME ON, LET'S GO!

HOW ABOUT HIM?

WE'LL GAG HIM AND TAKE HIM ALONG. HE MAY KNOW SOMETHING USEFUL.

GAULISH SPIES. IF I CAN CAPTURE THEM, IT MAY SAVE MY BACON!

I'M ON TO A GOOD THING!

ARE WE OFF, THEN?

WE'RE OFF!

CRAAASH!

CLANG!

NOT A SOUL!

LET'S GET OUT OF TOWN AND INTO THE FOREST.

TALK ABOUT A STROKE OF LUCK!

WE'LL BE ALL RIGHT HERE. AND NOW TO QUESTION THE GOTH!

IT'S COLD!

THIS REALLY IS INCREDIBLE!

DO YOU KNOW WHERE THE GAULISH DRUID IS?

Carry on, ask away!

HE DOESN'T SPEAK GAULISH... I NEVER THOUGHT OF THAT!

AAA-TISHOO!

BLESS YOU.

THANKS.

?!!?

?!!?

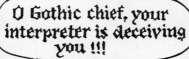

*This game, QUINQUIREMES AND GALLEYS, IS STILL PLAYED DURING LESSONS TODAY, THOUGH THE PLAYERS, IF DISCOVERED, MAY FIND THEMSELVES IN DIRE STRAITS.

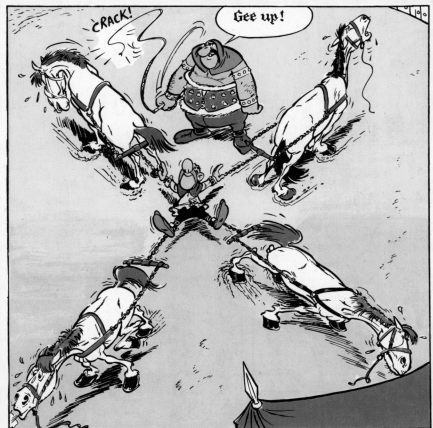

Now, everyone listen to me! I've got some of the Gaulish druid's magic powers! I'm your new chief, Rhetoric I!

That's the stuff! Down with Metric!

Hurrah! Long live Rhetoric I!

PLATCH!

CLAP! CLAP! CLAP!

Just a minute! I'm the chief around here!

Throw this poor fish into the dungeons! It's time you were going, Metric

SOON AFTERWARDS, IN THE PALACE...

COME ALONG IN, FRIENDS, COME ALONG IN. I WAS JUST PLANNING THE PROGRAMME FOR METRIC'S TORTURE TOMORROW.

What were we saying?

Well, and then we could put him in a double saucepan and stir over a slow flame...

SORRY TO INTERRUPT YOU, RHETORIC, BUT WE HAVE A FAVOUR TO ASK YOU...

YES? ANYTHING YOU LIKE, MY DEAR ASTERIX!

WE WANT TO VISIT METRIC IN HIS DUNGEON, TO CROW OVER HIM...

AN EXCELLENT IDEA! OFF YOU GO! HAVE A NICE TIME!

IT'S STILL WORKING!

When these Gauls have served their purpose I'll have to get rid of them...

I've got something special for them: a pressure cooker. It can cook a person in a couple of minutes, and it whistles when he's done!

Hee, hee! You can't stop progress!

ASTERIX, GETAFIX AND OBELIX MAKE THEIR WAY BACK TO THE DUNGEON FOR A WORD WITH METRIC...

Metric, would you like to get your revenge on Rhetoric and return to power?

?

HE SAYS YES!

I GOT THE GENERAL IDEA!

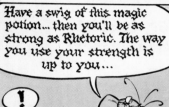

Have a swig of this magic potion... then you'll be as strong as Rhetoric. The way you use your strength is up to you...

!

GLUG! GLUG!

CLINNNK!

HE'S GOT A FREE HAND NOW!

CRAAAAASH!

Here we go again! They ought to replace that door by a curtain!

Raise the alarm! The prisoner's escaping!!!

So what?

POC!

HE'S GOT A FREE HAND! HA! HA! HA! THAT'S A GOOD ONE, THAT IS! I'VE ONLY JUST GOT IT. HO! HO! HO!

41

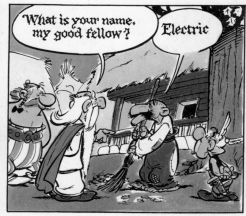

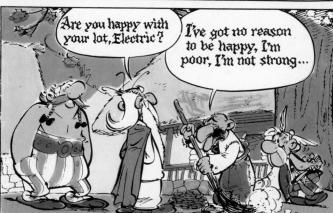

Metric

Rhetoric

THE ASTERIXIAN WARS
A Tangled Web...

The ruse employed by Asterix, Getafix and Obelix succeeded beyond their wildest dreams. After drinking the druid's magic potion, the Goths fought each other tooth and nail. Here is a brief summary to help you follow the history of these famous wars.

The favourite and devastating weapon of the combatants.

Diagram indicating the course of events.

The first victory is won outright by Rhetoric, who, having surprised Metric by an outflanking movement, lets him have it – bonk! – and inflicts a crushing defeat on him. This defeat, however, is only temporary ...

Rhetoric has no time to celebrate his victory, for, having completed his outflanking movement, he is taken in the rear by his own ally, Lyric. Lyric instantly proclaims himself supreme chief of all the Goths, much to the amusement of the other chiefs ....

Who turn out to be right, for Lyric's brother-in-law Satiric lays an ambush for him, pretending to invite him to a family reunion and Lyric falls into the trap. It was upon this occasion that the proposition that blood is thicker than water was first put to the test ...

Rhetoric goes after Lyric, with the avowed intention of "bashing him up" (archaic), but his rearguard is surprised by Metric's vanguard. Bonk! This manoeuvre is known as the Metric System.

General Electric manages to surprise Euphoric meditating on the conduct of his next few campaigns. Euphoric's morale is distinctly lowered, but he has the last word, with his famous remark, "I'll short-circuit him yet"

While Electric proclaims himself supreme chief of the Goths, to the amusement of all and sundry, it is the turn of Metric's rearguard to be surprised by Rhetoric's vanguard. Bonk! "This is bad for my system," is the comment of the exasperated Metric.

In fact, it is so bad for his system that he allows himself to be surprised by Euphoric. The battle is short and sharp. Euphoric, a wily politician, instantly proclaims himself supreme chief of the Goths. The other supreme chiefs are in fits ...

Euphoric, much annoyed, sets up camp and decides to sulk. He is surprised by Eccentric, who in his turn is attacked by Lyric, subsequently to be defeated by Electric. Electric is destined to be betrayed by Satiric, who will be beaten by Rhetoric.

Going round a corner, Rhetoric's vanguard bumps into Metric's vanguard. Bonk! Bonk! This battle is famous in the Asterixian wars as the "Battle of the Two Losers" And so the war goes on ...

MEANWHILE, OUR THREE FRIENDS ARE APPROACHING THE FRONTIER OF GAUL, WITH THEIR MINDS AT REST...

PRINTED IN BELGIUM BY

proost
INTERNATIONAL BOOK PRODUCTION